DAVE BURROWS

MONEY, WEALTH
AND THE
KINGDOM ECONOMY

TABLE OF CONTENTS

CHAPTER 1:

UNDERSTANDING MONEY AND WEALTH

What if I told you there is enough money and resources on Earth for every person to have more than enough for the rest of their lives? The truth is there is no shortage of resources on Earth. When the Earth was formed, everything to sustain all life was built in. God would not build something to run out or be lacking. He instituted a principle called **the principle of replenish**, which ensures that we should never run out of resources unless we destroy God's system through abuse and neglect. Every seed that produces a tree has seeds built in so that life is sustained forever. Every creature, great and small, possesses seeds to replenish so we would never run out of people or resources for the people to consume. The only fruit that does not replenish is "seedless" fruit. If you go to the grocery store today, there are seedless fruit. Any fruit that is seedless is a danger because it cannot replenish.

One of the most misunderstood subjects in the world is wealth and money. When we think of money and wealth, some obvious thoughts and statements come to mind. For example, "Money is the root of all evil." This misquoted scripture makes it appear that money itself is evil when the Bible actually says, "The <u>LOVE</u> of money is the root of all evil." This means the attachment and obsession with money is what produces evil. Another statement is, "It is easier for a camel to go through the eye of a needle than it is for a rich man to enter the Kingdom."

It makes it seem like it is nearly impossible for a rich man to enter the Kingdom. However, God Himself says that He made His servants rich, like Abraham and Solomon. Why would He make His people rich if it is so difficult for them to serve Him with health? Why would He tell Israel, "You will be the head and not the tail" and "You will lend and not borrow"? If we examine this statement more closely, we see that it refers to rich people consumed or attached to their money. On the surface, these statements seem to indicate that it is almost impossible to be good if you are rich, but a close review leads to clarification.

There is a difference between wealth and excess, and it is important to know the difference. If you have twenty-one cars but no one drives them, or if you have eighteen houses and no one lives in them, this is excess. **Money is meant to circulate and to serve us and not for us to serve it.** When money stops circulating, it causes financial constipation and mental illness.

The dictionary indicates that excess is "Exceeding a normal, usual, reasonable, or proper limit. ex•ces sive•ly adv. ex•ces sive•ness n. Synonyms: excessive, exorbitant, extravagant, immoderate, the state of exceeding what is normal or sufficient: rains that filled the reservoirs to excess. 2. An amount or quantity beyond what is normal or sufficient. Wealth is good, while excess is bad.

Perhaps this is why many have associated being poor with being holy or good. Some religious sects swear to a vow of poverty. Is money really bad, and does having money lead to bad outcomes? To answer these questions, we need a clear understanding of the purpose of money and wealth. If you understand the purpose of a thing, then it is easier to figure out the best use. Dr. Myles Munroe stated, "Where purpose is not known, abuse (abnormal use) is inevitable." **The greatest money problem in the world is when the wrong people possess it. There is no scripture in the Bible where God promises poverty, but there are many where He promises wealth or abundance.**

There is a scripture, 3 John 2, that states, "Beloved, I pray that you may prosper in all things and be in health, just as your soul prospers." So God, in His Word through the Apostle John, tells us that above all things, He wants us to prosper and be in good health just as or in proportion to our soul prospering. This is a clear indication of what God desires for us; He wants us to have, but He wants it to happen in the right context. He desires us to prosper and be in good health, <u>proportionate to our soul prospering</u>. This is important because if your soul is prospering, you will be kind, compassionate, and giving, and you will not be selfish and abusive. If your soul is not prospering, you will abuse your wealth, and people will suffer rather than benefit.

From the time of creation, God never added anything to Earth. When we think of God providing resources from heaven, it is not money being dropped from the sky. God does not drop provisions from the sky; He moves resources from one place to another on Earth. God does not give us money; He gives us trees that we can convert into money. God put furniture in the trees and gave us wisdom on how to extract it. God put everything in place, but man operating under a corrupt "world" system has distorted and destroyed God's economic system. No economic model in the world represents the Kingdom model. Communism, capitalism, socialism, and all the others are impotent models that blur the view of the Kingdom model. While we are quite aware of the shortcomings of communism and socialism, the idea that capitalism is a Kingdom model is untrue. In capitalist-driven societies, wealth is concentrated according to status, and people die every day simply because they lack the basic resources needed to sustain their lives. A billionaire can live a few blocks from the most destitute neighborhood yet do nothing to alleviate suffering when it is clearly within his power to do so. This is not the Kingdom economy.

Recently, it was announced that 12 billionaires in the USA are collectively worth over 1 trillion dollars. Twelve men are worth more than most countries in the world. At the same time, millions are out of work and have difficulty finding food and paying rent. People are starving to death in many countries, and yet others waste resources that could help the poor. Should there not be a balance between where resources go and where the needs are? What does this mean, and is this a part of God's design for the Earth and its economy? Is this the result of another system? I found myself asking these questions as soon as I saw the news clip about the increase in wealth of the billionaires. Is this something we should celebrate or be appalled by? I am not against having wealth and have no issue with wealth, but to accumulate massive amounts of wealth and the announcement not to be followed by massive donations to help those in suffering had me questioning if this is what Jesus spoke about when He talked about "mammon."

In capitalistic societies, people end up in hospitals and die because they do not have enough money for surgery or medication. I recently heard a story from a friend who complained that his wife was in an accident and went to the emergency room and was told the doctor would not operate until $25,000 was paid upfront. The person was sitting on a gurney in pain, and if they did not have this money upfront, they would be turned away and possibly die. It is unimaginable that rich people are given the best health care, and poor people are left on a gurney in pain because of money. Pharmaceutical and insurance companies deny benefits to aged persons when they need it most. The system is such that relatively few people become wealthy while millions suffer lack and deprivation. A powerful and startling truth is that between 1-2% of the world's population controls 99% of the world's resources.

A story by the BBC in 2016 reported that the richest 1% now has as much wealth as the rest of the world combined, according to Oxfam. It used **data from Credit Suisse** for the report, which urges leaders meeting in Davos (at the World Economic Forum) to take action on inequality. **Oxfam also calculated** that the richest 62 people in the world had as much wealth as the poorest half of the global population. It criticized the work of lobbyists and the amount of money kept in tax havens.

According to a report in the Global Citizen in 2023, **"81 billionaires have more wealth than 50% of the world combined."** There are six billionaires who together are worth over 1 trillion dollars. Very few economies in the world can boast of being worth 1 trillion dollars. To be exact, only 19 countries in the world have economies of over 1 trillion dollars. These men alone have more wealth than half of the world's poor population and more wealth than 175 out of 195 countries. Jeff Bezos and Elon Musk collectively are worth almost 400 billion dollars, while the entire GDP of some small countries is 8-12 billion. The Bahamas, where I am from, has an economy of just over 12 billion dollars (as of 2022).

Understanding is key to appropriating Kingdom wealth and the Kingdom economy. In the world, the natural inclination is self-preservation to maintain what you have, whereas in the Kingdom, it is the opposite. The one who gives ends up receiving more, and the one who withholds sees a decrease. This scripture makes it plain in Proverbs 11:24 NKJV: "There is one who scatters, yet increases more; And there is one who withholds more than is right, But it leads to poverty." It may not make sense to the natural mind, but the Kingdom economic system often runs counter to the systems of the world.

KEY KINGDOM WEALTH CONCEPTS

- **The principle of replenish** ensures that we technically should never run out of resources unless we destroy God's system through abuse and neglect.

- Every seed that produces a tree has seeds built in so that life is sustained forever.

- Every creature, great and small, possesses seeds to replenish so we would never run out of people or resources for the people to consume.

- **"The <u>LOVE</u> of money is the root of all evil," and not "Money is the root of all evil." This means the attachment and obsession with money is what produces evil.**

- **He desires us to prosper and be in good health, <u>proportionate to our soul prospering</u>.**

- God does not drop provisions from the sky; He moves resources from one place to another on Earth.

- God does not give us money; He gives us trees that we can convert into money.

- God put furniture in the trees and gave us wisdom on how to extract it.

- No economic model in the world represents the Kingdom model. Communism, capitalism, socialism, and all the others may have merits, but they are not the Kingdom economy model.

NOTES

_____

_____

_____

_____

_____

_____

_____

_____

_____

_____

_____

_____

_____

_____

CHAPTER 2:

KINGDOM ECONOMY VS MAMMON

To understand money and wealth, we must go to the words of Jesus, who explained that there are **only two systems** and **two options** that exist in the world: **mammon or Kingdom.** Mammon encompasses all economic models in the world to varying degrees. In Matthew 6:19-21 KJV, Jesus made this statement, "Do not lay up for yourselves treasures on Earth, where moth and rust destroy and where thieves break in and steal; but lay up for yourselves treasures in heaven, where neither moth nor rust destroys and where thieves do not break in and steal. For where your treasure is, there your heart will be also. **You cannot serve God and mammon.** "The lamp of the body is the eye. If, therefore, your eyes are good, your whole body will be full of light. But if your eye is bad, your whole body will be full of darkness. If, therefore, the light that is in you is darkness, how great *is* that darkness!" (Matthew 6:21-23). "No one can serve two masters; for either he will hate the one and love the other, or else he will be loyal to the one and despise the other (Matthew 6:24). **You cannot serve God (Kingdom) and mammon.**

Jesus associated money in the wrong context with the word called "mammon." When money is misunderstood or misused, it becomes mammon. The dictionary definition is as follows: "Mammon is a term derived from the Christian Bible, used to describe material wealth or greed, most often personified as a deity, and sometimes included in the seven princes of Hell. Etymologically, the word is assumed to derive from Late Latin 'mammon', from Greek 'μαμμωνάς', Syriac 'mámóna' (riches),[1] and was an Aramaic loan word in Hebrew meaning wealth[2] or possessions,[3] although it may also have meant 'that in which one trusts'.[4] The Greek word for "mammon", μαμμωνάς, occurs in the Sermon on the Mount (during the discourse on ostentation) and in the parable of the Unjust Steward (Luke 16:9-13).

Christians began to use the name of mammon as a pejorative, a term that was used to describe greed, avarice, and unjust worldly gain in biblical literature. It was personified as a false god in the New Testament. (Mt.6.24; Lk.16.13) The term is often used to refer to excessive materialism or greed as a negative influence.

This explanation shows us that God views the world system of money management and attitude as "mammon" and that it is in direct competition and conflict with His system. Jesus told His disciples about a widow who gave very little in monetary terms, but He considered her to have given more than all the rich people. This story is known as the "The Widow's Mite." It is possible in God's economy to give little and yet give more than the richest persons.

The Prodigal Son is another story that compares God's system with the world's. The point that Jesus made is that the prodigal son was already rich; he had access already given to him to wealth, but he wanted it in his hands. This is a classic example of Kingdom wealth vs mammon. The prodigal son became greedy and obsessed with taking his wealth and consuming it for his lusts. Jesus taught about economy but not like the average person; He brought a contrasting and superior understanding based upon the Kingdom economy.

My conclusion is that Jesus was saying there are only two economic systems in the world: the Kingdom economy and mammon. I also surmised that there are only two purposes for money and wealth:

1. Meet needs (and some desires)

2. Establish and advance the Kingdom on Earth (which in turn ensures that everyone has their needs met, at least basic needs)

When you receive or achieve wealth, you can consume it on your lusts and pleasures and get to the point where you can have billions of dollars in the bank while your neighbors starve. You can also achieve wealth and ensure that everyone around you has a better life because you are a good steward of resources. In the Old Testament, God stated, **"I have given you the power to get wealth to establish the covenant"** (Deuteronomy 8.18). This scripture indicates that wealth is not to be worshiped or used for selfish pursuits; it is for meeting your needs and the needs of others and then advancing the Kingdom to ensure that everyone's life improves. It does not mean you cannot have money for personal enjoyment. There are enough resources for you to not only have your needs met but also enjoy entertainment, homes, cars, vacations, and clothes. The important thing is that you consume within the Kingdom economy and use Kingdom economy principles rather than mammon-based consumption.

From Jesus' words, if one becomes consumed with wealth, they could end up serving "mammon," which results in thousands of people being homeless, people dying because they cannot afford health care and basic needs, while others sail around on yachts and private jets. He clearly indicated that this was not a system He endorsed; it was not and is not God's plan. Capitalism has its good points in terms of spurring innovation and causing people to strive to achieve, but **capitalism is not a Kingdom economic model.** If we look at God's system, which Jesus talked about, we will notice that He believes in being fruitful, multiplying, investing, and bringing returns, but not a system where people are deprived and dying. This system of hoarding and not circulating money is called **financial constipation,** where tons of money is backed up in a corner and not circulating. Mammon is when a drug can cost $5.00 and is sold to poor people at $100 to $200. This is what a "mammon" attitude can do.

How does mammon contrast with the "Kingdom economy?" I believe in the Kingdom economy. Jesus would consider health-care a need, not a luxury, and housing and food a need, not a luxury. There are countries in the world where citizens do not have to pay for health care and some countries where even utilities are provided. The greatest problem with wealth in the world today is not a lack of resources; the problem is who has the wealth and who they are serving. Food is a need; housing is a need; health-care is a need. Every government in the world should automatically provide these necessities to those who cannot afford them with the stipulation that if they can work, they should work for it because God is a God of productivity. The popular scriptural refrain found in 2 Thessalonians 3:10 (New King James Version):

"For even when we were with you, we commanded you this: If anyone will not work, neither shall he eat." The clear indicator is that if you can work, you should work to provide for your family.

Productivity should always be tied to provision as long as the person is able-bodied. The truth about life is that if people have their basic needs met, they are much more productive, and it is easier for countries to function. It actually becomes better for business because no one is idle. The dictionary definition of mammon is **"wealth regarded as an evil influence or false object of worship and devotion."**

Mammon is a system where some countries have nothing because their leaders hoard the resources while the people die of starvation. If people's needs are met, it is easier for economies to function and for people to be successful in business. In the Kingdom system, no one lacks, and no one is unproductive. There is nothing wrong with businesses making reasonable profits and accumulating wealth; the problem begins when you acquire wealth, and your 'God' is mammon. I am a business owner and an investor, and I believe in being rewarded for your hard work. No good thing comes from a god called mammon because it is the worship of money and is under the administration of the devil.

So my question to you today is, what type of mentality do you have? You do not have to be rich to have a mammon mentality. The poor man, who hates the rich in many cases, would love to trade places and would do the very same thing the rich are doing. Many poor people are envious of the rich and want to be in their place where they will act the same way as the rich person. During seasons of great financial distress, each of us should look inside and ensure that we help those in need within our capabilities.

What are you doing to help others during difficult seasons? If you hold onto something that you should give away, that's mammon. If you are in a position to help and you do not help, that is mammon. Let us all remember to be our brother and sister's keeper and not become a victim of mammon. In my life, I have given away four cars, countless dollars (in proportion to my personal wealth), vacation trips, and paid bills for persons in need without ever advertising it. I consider it a reasonable service and a part of the Kingdom economy. The world needs people interested in distribution, circulation, and helping rather than hoarding.

Mammon is based on the ideas and purpose of man (under the jurisdiction of a system called the World, under the "God of this world"). One of the features of mammon is **financial constipation**. Mammon is designed as a master to be worshiped instead of God and holds its adherents in bondage where they may achieve wealth but not abundant life or happiness. Mammon is characterized by self-indulgence, consumption, and excess. The system of mammon encourages individuals to acquire resources and hoard them so that they never circulate. There are rich people in the world who own houses and yachts and fly around the world and would see one of their people destitute (including persons who work for them) and do not help. Mammon has resources backed up in corners away from people who need the resources. Jesus said, you will either serve God or mammon; you will love and serve one, but you cannot do both.

KEY KINGDOM ECONOMY PRINCIPLES

- There are **only two systems** and **two options** that exist in the world: **mammon or Kingdom.**

- When money is misunderstood or misused, it becomes mammon.

- There are only two purposes for money and wealth: a) to meet needs (and some desires) and b) to establish and advance the Kingdom on Earth.

- This system of hoarding and not circulating money is called **financial constipation** (where tons of money is backed up in a corner and not circulating).

- Productivity should always be tied to provision as long as the person is able-bodied.

- The world needs people who are interested in distribution, circulation, and helping rather than hoarding.

NOTES

CHAPTER 3:

UNDERSTANDING MONEY AND WEALTH; THE KINGDOM ECONOMY

The Kingdom economy is built upon the principle of circulation. In the Kingdom economy, no one lacks or is destitute because those who have shared their wealth voluntarily with those who do not. This model was introduced in the Book of Acts. The scripture shows that persons even sold their possessions and distributed them to those in need. Acts 4:32-35; "Now the multitude of those who believed were of one heart and one soul; neither did anyone say that any of the things he possessed was his own, but **they had all things in common.** And with great power, the apostles gave witness to the resurrection of the Lord Jesus. And great grace was upon them all. **Nor was there anyone among them who lacked**; for all who were possessors of lands or houses sold them, and brought the proceeds of the things that were sold, and laid *them* at the apostles' feet; and they distributed to each as anyone had need."

The way the Kingdom economy works is that those who have help those who do not have, whether it is from an individual or corporate basis. The church (Kingdom Embassy) is designed ideally as a distribution center. This is God's economic system. Each person works and invests in building wealth; they use their wealth to establish the Kingdom through the church, which serves as the **distribution center**. This is God's design.

The tithe is simply a built-in system to ensure that resources are available for the upkeep of the House of Worship (Embassy), the pastors and staff members are taken care of, and everything else is distributed according to needs. No one would lack; everyone would have their needs met. This idea is genius because it comes from the mind of God. The problem is not that God did not give us a perfect plan; the problem is that people who say they are Christians refuse to operate according to the Kingdom economy, so the church often does not have enough to pay the bills and finds it difficult to help those in need because the people who are supposed to be submitted to the King are either ignorant or second-guessing the Word of God and opting to follow the system of mammon. If Christians and the Church operated according to God's economic plan, their communities would have no period of need or lack.

I have had friends who are sinners who say to me you are foolish for paying tithes until I explained to them that **everyone pays tithes and gives offerings**, even persons who have never been to a church. He insisted that he did no such thing. I asked him what he thinks happens when he goes to the local bar or the street corner to buy alcohol or drugs. "You are paying tithes to advance the Kingdom of Darkness." I made a joke to my friend that I used to receive tithes all the time when I was on the street corner as a supplier of exotic plants and pharmaceuticals. Men and women would line up to pay their tithes every day, especially on payday.

I gave another example relating to strip clubs. I told him that men would continually give **"rain" offerings** in the strip club. In strip clubs, patrons would often "make it rain" by throwing money up in the air when a stripper was performing. I told him this was the "rain offering" to the devil. So, if you are going to pay tithes and give offerings anyway, it is much better to direct it to advance the Kingdom than to a stripper or drug dealer. Jesus put it this way, "Wherever your heart is, your treasure will follow."

The Kingdom economy is the perfect economy and is already established. Unfortunately, Kingdom citizens live in ignorance and do not recognize that God has already built a perfect economic model, and if they followed it, there would be no lack. Another principle of the Kingdom economy is found in **Luke 6.38, "Give and it shall be given unto you, pressed down shaken together and running over shall men give unto you."** This is a Kingdom economic principle. Rather than hoarding, if everyone operates by this principle, money and wealth will circulate, and 'ALL' needs will be met.

Recently, a member of my church, a businessman, came to me and stated that he had finally received a revelation about wealth and money. He indicated that he was giving to persons who had approached him with needs and selecting causes to give to when it finally occurred to him that all he needed to do was give directly to the church and direct persons who were in need to the church. He did not have to deal with the administration of giving and distribution. **He told me that he realized that the church is the distribution center.** From that moment, he began to give resources to the church, and he directed people who were in need to the church. The church had a system of vetting that ensured the needs were legitimate and released him from a burden.

The way he gave before, in some cases, he was "casting pearl before swine." I will give you an example. He gave to people based on their stories of need and did not have time to check and verify that what they were saying was true. Some persons received donations under false pretenses, so the Kingdom economy was perverted. The same person came to the church asking for financial relief for furniture damaged in a hurricane. Our staff went out and did an inspection only to realize that the person asking for the money did not have any furniture damage and was dishonestly accumulating resources from believers who thought they were doing a good deed. The reason everything was brought to the apostles for distribution is that this is God's system of accountability. The story of Ananias and Sapphira in the Book of Acts is an example of the checks and balances that God built into His system. This couple lied about their giving, but this was found out by the apostles, and they ended up being struck down.

It is important for believers to realize that you cannot go wrong when you invest in the Kingdom economy. Investment in the Kingdom economy is not just about money. I would like to share a story about a Kingdom investment with you. My daughter Davrielle invested in the Kingdom over the years by serving in the church and mentoring inner-city girls since she was 15 years old. She was faithful but was not seeing the return she had expected as a faithful believer. She continued serving and being faithful despite friends telling her that good girls finish last and that she should join the crowd and not be a virtuous girl.

A young man in the church, Drew, also did his best to serve God, but he was not seeing the result he had expected. He was hearing the same noise about trying to live righteously. Having reached the 30-year-old mark, they both decided to seek the Kingdom. In her case, she continued serving by mentoring young ladies, and in his case, he had just returned from college and decided to take some time off to pray and to serve to help the church improve.

He was a video and production expert, and one day, he asked his dad, who is a close friend of mine, to meet with me to discuss how to improve the church services. He shared some thoughts and produced some video clips on what he felt could be improved. I welcomed the information and arranged a meeting with 150 of our leaders. He presented his thoughts. I was excited, and after the presentation, he left it at that. I told him we needed his expertise to assist with the process and decided to hire him on a contract for one year to help us improve. He also noted that we needed improvements in our worship ministry, and being a professional singer, he offered to help.

He formed a worship team and began recruiting some younger singers, and my daughter happened to be a professional singer. He ended up picking her up for practice, and what happened next was a story of blessing and favor. They both invested in the Kingdom and today, they are married and have received tremendous returns to the point where their individual careers have skyrocketed. They have received massive financial rewards, doubling, tripling, and even quadrupling their income above what they were receiving before. Their company also experienced exponential growth, and in just over one year, they were able to be the owners of their own home in a prestigious gated community.

To further understand the Kingdom economy, it is based upon these components (in no particular order):

- **Tithes and offerings** - God's model for ensuring provisions are available. This takes care of bills, salaries, upkeep, and capital development. It provides funding for programs and missions so that the pastors and the church can focus on ministry and not on fundraising. If tithes and offerings are not paid, how would a church get funds to sustain itself? Tithes are obviously a Kingdom economy model.

- **Seedtime and harvest** are eternal principles that ensure that abundance is perpetuated. Seeds always bear fruit, whether it is in the physical realm, financial realm, or spiritual realm. Nothing grows without a seed going into the ground. God Himself stated that as long as the Earth remains, there will be seedtime and harvest. If God says something, we need to obey and observe rather than second guess or fight against it. We should be people of seed and harvest. Some church leaders misrepresent this principle and use it as a point of coercion. I do not respond to coercion; I plant seeds solely based on my personal conviction and the direction I receive in my spirit from God.

- **Replenish** - Everything has been built into it, including the ability to continue supplying. The mind of God never allows for lack, and God builds sustainment into the source. He is the source and sustainer, and He will never run out, so whatever He creates shares His DNA and acts the same way. He told Adam and Eve to multiply and replenish because it was built into them. We should always be aware of and operate in this principle in every aspect of life.

- **Productivity** - Every person on Earth is supposed to work and to be fruitful and multiply. God built us to be productive, and He does not approve of laziness or idleness. Productivity is beneficial, and work is an essential component of life. Productivity improves our lives. In fact, productivity is related to health. Whatever does not move dies, whether it is the physical body or the mind. Exercise produces better health because we move. We should automatically think about productivity and be excited about being productive. Jesus actually cursed a fig tree that was not productive.

- **Investment** - If we look at the parables of Jesus, we often see examples of investment. One of the most prominent examples is what is known as the parable of the talents. Jesus showed in this parable that investment is a Kingdom economy principle, not based upon what one has but on what one does with what one has. Investment is God's plan for increase. Investment is a key component of the Kingdom economy.

- **Commonwealth** - In a Kingdom, the source of all wealth is the King, and he ensures equitable distribution when citizens abide by Kingdom economic policies. He promised to supply all of our needs, which is what a benevolent King does. Another prominent principle in the Bible is fairness and equitable distribution. When wealth is common, it means we can all access it through the King and the system He created.

- **Supernatural supply** - God moves and shifts based upon His established principles. Faith is the currency of the Kingdom economy. God moves and shifts according to the exercise of our faith. When we have a need and follow the protocols He established, money moves in ways that are not natural.

Through this principle, needs are met, and bills are paid outside of traditional sources, and the only explanation is that God did it.

KEY KINGDOM ECONOMY PRINCIPLES

- The Kingdom economy is built upon the principle of circulation.

- The way the Kingdom economy works is that those who have help those who do not have, whether on an individual or corporate basis.

- The church (Kingdom Embassy) is designed ideally as a distribution center.

- The tithe is simply a built-in system to ensure that resources are available for the upkeep of the House of Worship (the Embassy), the pastors and staff members are taken care of, and everything else is distributed according to needs. As such, no one would lack, and everyone would have their needs met.

- If Christians and the church operated according to God's economic plan, their communities would have no period of need or lack.

- **Everyone pays tithes and gives offerings**, even persons who have never been to a church (they give 10% minimum to what they value, whether it is the local bar, the club, the dope dealer--, or the golf club)

The Kingdom economy operates through:

- **Tithes and offerings**
- **Seedtime and harvest**
- **Replenish**
- **Productivity**
- **Investment**
- **Commonwealth**
- **Supernatural supply**

NOTES

CHAPTER 4:

THE PURPOSE OF WEALTH

What is the purpose of wealth from a Kingdom perspective? Does God favor sinners and expect them to be wealthy and Kingdom citizens to be poor? Is money supposed to be worshiped and consumed for pleasure and excess? To determine the purpose of wealth, we must always go back to the original, the one who created everything, and examine what He says about it in order to figure out its purpose.

The purpose of wealth is summed up in this statement in Deuteronomy 8:18 NKJV, "And you shall remember the Lord your God, for it is **He who <u>gives you power to get wealth</u>, (why) that He may establish His covenant which He swore to your fathers, as** it is **this day."**

The purpose of wealth is to establish God's covenant and His Kingdom on Earth because when His Kingdom is established in an environment, everything works, and people are happy. We know that Jesus prayed, "Thy Kingdom come, thy will be done on earth as it is in Heaven," which means it did not exist, and it would be beneficial if it did exist on Earth. The verse in Deuteronomy says He gives us **power (ability)** to get wealth so that it can be used to establish His covenant. His covenant includes loving God, loving your neighbor as yourself, giving to those in need, taking care of widows, be generous and kind. These virtues of the Kingdom are beneficial to all, and when persons who share these values have wealth, everyone benefits. The Bible puts it this way, **"When the righteous are in power, the people rejoice"** (Proverbs 29:2). There ought to be a sense of relief when the righteous have wealth because it means money will circulate and find its way to where the needs are. When God's Kingdom economy is working, everyone feels better because they know they will be treated fairly and no one will be **destitute.**

God wants you to prosper, especially if you are a part of His Kingdom. He said in Matthew 7:11, **"If you then, being evil, know how to give good gifts to your children, how much more will your Father who is in heaven give good things to those who ask Him!"** 'How much more will your father who is in heaven give good gifts to His children?' This is an indication that He wants us to have the best and wants to take care of us as a priority and not as an afterthought. The church is sometimes guilty of giving the impression that God wants sinners to have money and His children to suffer in need. Nothing can be further from the truth.

I believe that when you are a good person, and your soul is right, you deserve it! God wants you to prosper, and there is a specific reason He wants you to prosper. There is a purpose behind wealth and money. What is the purpose? The purpose is to establish the covenant (sacred agreement), which establishes the Kingdom, and wherever the Kingdom is, there is both liberty and abundance. I believe there is something we should know about money and resources on Earth. The Earth and things in it were designed to be self-sustaining. Trees bear fruit that have seeds that can create more trees, which will produce fruit and give more seeds that produce trees with fruit. Everything for Earth is already on Earth. Everything to sustain Earth is already on Earth. **God does not drop things from the sky; when we need something, it simply moves from one location on Earth to another to get to us.**

When we look at Jesus' actions when He needed money for taxes, He did not say let's pray and ask the Father to send from Heaven. What He did was tell the disciples to get it from the mouth of a fish. It was already on Earth, and it just needed to change locations so their taxes could be paid. **Everything you need is here (near), and when it gets to you, you need to keep and increase it using wisdom (knowledge of the Kingdom). Proverbs 16.16 states, "How much better to get wisdom than gold, to get insight rather than silver!**

When people understand the purpose of wealth, they ensure that their own needs are met, and after their needs are met, they look for others to help. People who understand the purpose of wealth know that God's house should be taken care of as a priority, and He will take care of our houses. The Bible plainly tells us to bring the tithe into the storehouse (Embassy) so that members (Kingdom citizens) can have their needs met. People who don't understand the purpose of wealth tend to consume extravagantly themselves and to hoard and hide money where it does not reach those in need. We all need money to survive, and that is why most of us go to work every day; we need to have our basic needs met. God wants us to have our needs met, but He also wants us to understand that after our needs are met, He has established some priorities. What are those priorities:

1. **Meet your needs** (and reasonable desires) – God promised to supply our needs according to His resources. Needs are needs. If you have children, you count it a privilege to make sure that your children have good to eat, a place to stay, and the basics of life. God is the same way with us; He wants us to have our needs met.

2. **Finance the Truth** – Because if lies are financed, then the world is captured and enslaved by philosophies and behavior that are against God and result in violence, crime, and corruption.

1 Peter 1:2; "Grace and peace be multiplied to you in the knowledge of God and of Jesus our Lord, as His divine power has given to us all things that *pertain* to life and godliness, through the knowledge of Him who called us by glory and virtue, by which have been given to us exceedingly great and precious promises, that through these you may be partakers of the divine nature, having escaped the corruption *that is* in the world through lust."

3. **Establish the Kingdom** – This means to introduce 'man' to his spiritual connection to God (The King) and, as a result of this connection, establish a pattern of behavior and culture that is in line with what is good and right, following the example of Jesus who came to show us how to live. Establishing the Kingdom is a return to God's original plan for man.

Wherever the Kingdom is advanced, the people automatically benefit at an optimum level. God is a **benevolent** King, which means He looks out for and ensures the well-being of His citizens, unlike many earthly kings. Many kings of the Earth have people serving them and working hard to give more them. The king lives in opulence, while the citizens may be homeless or destitute with inadequate housing, healthcare, and resources. The King of England and other kings of the Earth would often colonize countries by forcibly taking them over and enslaving the populations to work for the king and send resources back to him.

I am from the Bahamas, and slaves were taken from Africa by the British Monarchy and transported here specifically to work cotton fields, sugar cane fields, and other resources, which were then shipped back to Britain. The slaves were not paid and were severely abused. This is what a malevolent King does; he looks out for himself at the expense of the citizens. God, on the other hand, is a benevolent King, and He looks out for everyone. No one is a slave to the King; everyone is treated fairly and appropriately. It was not just England that did this. Kings and emperors of Asia, the Middle East, and Africa all operated under this principle, and some still do even to this day. In the Kingdom of God, no one works to give riches to the King. The King gives principles on how resources should be distributed and shared and ensures that no one lives in lack.

KEY KINGDOM ECONOMY PRINCIPLES

- The purpose of wealth is to establish God's covenant and His Kingdom on Earth because when His Kingdom is established in an environment, everything works, and people are happy.

- God wants you to prosper, especially if you are a part of His Kingdom.

- When people understand the purpose of wealth, they ensure that their own needs are met, and after their needs are met, they look for others to help.

- People who understand the purpose of wealth know that God's house should be taken care of as a priority, and He will take care of our houses.

- Wherever the Kingdom is advanced, the people automatically benefit at an optimum level.

- God is a **benevolent** King, which means He looks out for and ensures the well-being of His citizens, unlike many earthly kings.

NOTES

CHAPTER 5:

HOW MONEY MOVES

As I stated previously, everything for Earth is already on Earth, so the only thing that needs to happen to money is that it needs to move and circulate. Resources that are abundant in one place and lacking in another just need to move to where the need is. Essentially, money and resources need to move so that there is balance, and the resources end up where the needs are. If there are poor people with no food in Africa and there is one man with 5 billion dollars of resources in America, **we do not have a poverty problem; we have a distribution problem.** There are many cities that I have been in around the world where there is one community that is gated with luxurious homes, and then a block away, there is abject poverty. It does not mean that resources should be taken from one community and given to another; resources should naturally move to where the need is because leaders who know how to operate on Kingdom principles are in place.

I am not speaking of forcible redistribution of wealth; I am speaking of the Kingdom principle, where resources go to where needs are naturally through leadership observation of Kingdom principles. Man has never fully grasped this concept, even though there have been attempts to do so. This is where communism, socialism, and capitalism have come from, as well as attempts to spread wealth. The problem is that when the root of the system is mammon, it self-destructs despite the best intentions.

God built a system where seeds are built in to replenish, to never run out, so resources are always available in perpetuity. If man gains an understanding of how resources move in the Kingdom, the issues would go away, and we would have both peace and abundance on the Earth. Let's examine how money moves and how to ensure that we observe Kingdom economy principles in our lives.

Remember that there are only two types of economies:

1. Mammon (man-made economies – capitalism, communism, consumerism)
2. Kingdom economy

There are four things that make money move:

- Ideas
- Talent
- Seedtime and Harvest
- Favor and Blessing

IDEAS

Let's begin with **IDEAS**. Every rich person on Earth becomes rich as a result of an idea. They may end up passing their wealth on to others, but the basis of their wealth is usually an idea. This idea can be an innovation, a solution to a problem, or a repositioning of an existing idea. If we take a look at the wealthiest people in the world, we will see this common thread: Amazon is simply an idea. Brick-and-mortar stores existed for years, but one man came up with an idea to change the way we do shopping, and he became rich. In most cases, the persons who come up with these ideas are not wealthy; **wealth and money run after them**. Steve Jobs, the founder of Apple Computers, was a college dropout with the idea of creating something that never existed: the personal computer. Within a few years of sharing this idea, millions and millions of dollars pursued him. Facebook is an idea. The founder, Mark Zuckerberg, was just a college student until he came up with this idea for social media. Microsoft was an idea in the head of Bill Gates, and money ran him down. The list is endless. Money follows ideas. Rich people, investment companies, and banks are looking for ideas to invest in. When an idea with potential shows up, money runs toward it. If you want to be successful in life, one of the most important things you can do is to keep thinking and searching for ideas that will end up attracting wealth. **Money is a vehicle that transports ideas.**

Ideas come in many forms; let's look at repositioning ideas. Uber does not own any vehicles, but it has one of the largest fleets of vehicles in the world. They took an existing idea and repositioned it, which resulted in enormous wealth. Airbnb changed the lodging business and made many people wealthy. They do not own hotels, but they had an idea to use a software model allowing people to use their homes in the same way that one uses a hotel. They do not own the homes; they own the idea. It is the idea that generates wealth for them. The smartphone took something that was already in popular use and changed the dynamics, resulting in massive wealth shifts for companies like Samsung and Apple.

If you are old enough to recall, Blackberry was the king of the smartphone, and the iPhone was dismissed. Years later, this generation has no idea what a Blackberry is. If you think about it, when Jesus said to Peter, "Throw your net on the other side," it was a repositioning. Ideas are guaranteed to make money move. The Book of Proverbs speaks of God giving us ideas for "Witty Inventions": Proverbs 8:12 KJV: I wisdom dwells with prudence, and find out knowledge of witty inventions. Keep searching for ideas rather than money.

TALENT

The second thing that makes money move is **TALENT**. Have you ever noticed that people with money go after talented people? To give you a few examples, why would someone pay an entertainer or an athlete $250 million? The reason is that people will part with money for talent. If you take away talent, then no one is interested in those people. If they get injured, money stops chasing them because the owners of money chase talent, and dormant talent that is not on display does not generate revenue.

A man who bounces a ball can make more money than 99.95 percent of the people in America because of his talent. Athletes globally are now signing multi-billion dollar contracts because of their talent. European football clubs (Soccer) have some of the highest-paid athletes in the world. The only reason they are able to make this money is because of their talent. Have you ever noticed how, after the Olympics, the winners get massive endorsement deals? When their talent produces a gold medal, and people are able to view the performer face to face, they compete for their services and sometimes get into a bidding war. If the same athlete loses the next year, then the same monied people will go after the more recent success story and ignore the former. **One key to wealth is to look inside and see what talents you were born with and develop those talents, understanding that it is those talents that might make the difference between financial success and failure for you.** Whatever your talent is is what will make you money. The Bible puts it this way, "Your gift (talent) will make room for you and take you before kings." **Proverbs 18:16 NKJV: "A man's gift makes room for him, and brings him before great men (kings)." Dr. Myles Munroe came from an impoverished inner-city community where expectations were low, but he ended up in the presence of kings and world leaders because of his gift. To this day, people all over the world, including presidents and prime ministers, still visit or call me because of their appreciation for him. It is not him that they gravitate to; it is his gift that attracts people. What is your gift (talent)?**

A mechanic who is talented at fixing cars generates income, an accountant who is talented with figures generates income, a runner, an artist, and anyone with talent generates money, and money follows them. The more talented you are, the more money follows you. The key to resources flowing to you is discovering and developing your talent.

SEEDTIME AND HARVEST

This is sometimes referred to as sowing and reaping. Whatever you sow, you tend to reap. Whatever you invest in is what will bring you your return. If you want to make money, find something to plant that is fruitful, and money will be yours. A farmer who plants corn reaps financial reward when the harvest comes. Even intangible things, when they are planted, bring about a return. The Bible tells us that if you want friends, be friendly. This means you plant the seed of friendship by being friendly, and once that seed is watered, you reap a harvest of friendship.

Your harvest is related to your seed. If you plant love, love tends to come back to you multiplied. You can find this principle throughout the Bible. Seedtime and harvest must become a lifestyle and not something that is turned on and off on occasion. A farmer lives by the seed principle. He or she realizes that you cannot grow without a seed, and you cannot expect a seed to grow without being planted. You cannot expect the planted seed to succeed if it is not placed in the right soil. A smart farmer does not indiscriminately plant or spread seeds. He strategically places it in the right environment based on the type of seed and the harvest he wants to receive. It is important to know what good soil is, what bad soil is, and what the right timing for seed is. A seed planted out of season and in the wrong environment will not produce the desired result.

I look for good soil (environment) when planting my seed. I did not just give away cars indiscriminately; each time I gave away a car, I gave to someone who needed a car but also someone who was actively engaged in advancing the Kingdom. If I gave it without purpose, the person I gave it to could have taken that car and used it to commit crimes or transport drugs or some other nefarious purpose. In one case, it was a single mother who assisted in the youth ministry and had lost her vehicle. In another case, it was a friend who was experiencing a major financial struggle. I knew that they could not afford a vehicle. I also knew that they had served faithfully in ministry, so I purposefully put my resources in the right environment to accomplish the Kingdom's purpose, meet a need, and advance the Kingdom.

FAVOR AND BLESSING

Favor is defined in Merriam-Webster's dictionary as "a special privilege or right granted or conceded." Another definition of favor is "an act of kindness beyond what is due or usual." Essentially, a favor is something that is not deserved or sometimes even expected or anticipated. It shows up, and you benefit. The favor of God is one of those things that will sometimes show up, and the only explanation is that God caused something to happen for you that cannot be explained logically. There are times when things happen financially that do not follow any logic; you did not do anything to deserve it; it was not part of your expectation, and the only explanation is that God decided to favor you by moving resources in a way and through a channel that is not normal.

Every Sunday, I ask my congregation to repeat a confession that they have come to love and even request and insist that I do it every week. The confession is, **"Today, I expect favor, preferential treatment, unusual blessings, and abundant provisions and resources."** I explain to them that favor comes from God, and we should expect to be favored because He is a benevolent King, and He conveys favor to His children. The scripture speaks of Him doing, "Exceedingly, abundantly above all we ask or think all that we could ask, think or imagine" (Ephesians 3:20). This means we can and should expect the unusual blessings that come with being the child of a benevolent King.

I have been the beneficiary of favor on many occasions, and at this point, my attitude is where the favor is coming from next, not if it is coming. One day, out of the blue, I looked into my bank account online, and I saw a very substantial amount transferred to me. I did not ask for the money. I was not very close to the person who sent the money, and I could not explain why they did it for me. There are times when God inspires someone to do something on your behalf that is not a result of your talent, any seed you planted, or any idea you presented; it just showed up supernaturally. When you are operating in the Kingdom lifestyle, the Bible says God will cause men to give into your bosom. When God does it, it is favor and blessing, and it is supernatural in origin.

I can recall another time I was checking an online giving site for our church, and a substantial gift showed up in the name of the wife of a multi-million dollar athlete. I asked some of my team members if they knew the athlete or his wife, but no one knew her. It only happened on one occasion, and there was no note or explanation. This meant to me that it was not a logical or normal gift. This individual was impressed supernaturally, and they obeyed the Holy Spirit and delivered what they were told to deliver.

I can recall another incident where a ministry and school owed over 100 million dollars in debt, and a very rich man from a prominent business family decided to give them the 100 million. Can you imagine one day someone deciding to give you 100 million dollars? This is supernatural favor and blessing in operation. Money moves as the Holy Spirit leads, and people become the beneficiaries. There is nothing you can do to get people to act in this manner, and many times, we have no idea who the people are and when they will decide to give to us. It is from an entirely different realm than normal economics. Favor and supernatural giving often come with no request, connection, or return address. It is just the supernatural favor of God.

KEY KINGDOM ECONOMY PRINCIPLES

· If there are poor people with no food in Africa and there is one man with 5 billion dollars of resources in America, **we do not have a poverty problem; we have a distribution problem.**

· God built a system where seeds are built in to replenish, to never run out, so resources are always available in perpetuity.

· **Money is a vehicle that transports ideas.**

There are four things that make money move:

• Ideas
• Talent
• Seedtime and Harvest
• Favor and Blessing

NOTES

_____

_____

_____

_____

_____

_____

_____

_____

_____

_____

_____

_____

_____

_____

_____

_____

CHAPTER 6:

KINGDOM ECONOMIC PRINCIPLES

Everything in the world operates by principles or rules. When you think of science, medicine, or economics, there are principles that govern their operation. Gravity is a principle. There is no Christian gravity and sinner gravity. Gravity is a principle of life, and if you obey the principle, you benefit. If you defy the principle, you become a victim. If you obey the rules, you benefit; if you go against the rules, you suffer. The Kingdom has economic principles that govern its operation on the Earth. What follows is a list of key principles of the Kingdom economy.

1. PRODUCTIVITY

God made man to produce. He said in the beginning that we are to be fruitful and multiply. When humans are not productive, they deteriorate physically, mentally, and spiritually. If you look at the design of 'man,' especially males, you can tell that they are designed to work and be productive. A man, by physical design, is built for physical tasks. That does not mean he is not built to work mentally, but the physical aspect is the most obvious. To be fruitful and multiply does not apply to just having children. **Fruitful and multiplying also means engaging your God-given resources in a productive manner to fulfill His mandate.**

The worst thing that can happen to a man (or woman) is to be idle. We were designed to be continually active and productive. When we are idle, we invite trouble, and it produces a lethargy that reconditions the mind and affects the psyche. Idle people are more prone to hopelessness and are attracted to schemes. Idle people are more prone to substance abuse and crime. Staying productive is essential for survival in the Kingdom economy. Whatever does not move dies; this is true in the physical and mental realm. Years ago, there used to be a commercial for HB-CUs (Historically Black Colleges and Universities) that stated, "A mind is a terrible thing to waste." The commercial was asking for donors to help students attend college so that their minds could be put to productive use. Without this, they would be idle and deteriorate.

One of the things I always tell young men who come to me seeking jobs is that they should not seek a job first but seek to be productive. I will give you an example. A young man came to me looking for a job, and I asked him what his interests and skills were. After he told me what his interests and skills were, I instructed him to work in our media department for free. Most people would say, "Why would you ask someone to go and work and not be paid?" The answer is that if they stay at home, there is no movement or advancement; they are just idle. On the other hand, if they are productive in their area of interest, they are actually increasing their value for the future. Essentially, they are working for free, but their work is paying them back by allowing them to acquire knowledge and refine skills that will become valuable in the future.

The young man in question worked in the media department and understudied the video producer. Eventually, after a year or so, the video producer left to pursue another opportunity. When we were looking for a replacement, where was the first place we looked? We looked at the person who was already doing the job. We hired him, and eventually, his skills improved to the point where he was recruited by others who were paying more money. He accepted another job that paid more than we could, and while on that job, another firm in Canada saw his work and invited him to work in Canada. Today, he has his own company in Canada and is thriving because he has decided to be productive rather than waiting for a salary.

This is why I believe even if persons are on welfare or being given money, there should be a work requirement. If there is no work requirement, they can receive money, sit on the corner and play dominoes, or do drugs all day and develop atrophy. Productivity is essential to life in the Kingdom, which is why the Bible states that if a man does not work, he should not eat. Productivity is the first pillar of the Kingdom economy.

2. INVESTMENT

The second pillar of the Kingdom economy is investment. Investment does not only relate to money. You can invest money, you can invest time, you can invest love, you can invest in spiritual things. Jesus actively taught the principle of investment. **Investment is not about what you have; it is about what you**

do with what you have. Here we see Jesus telling a story about investment:

"For it will be like a man going on a journey, who called his servants and entrusted to them his property. ^{15} To one he gave five talents, to another two, to another one, to each according to his ability. Then he went away. ^{16} He who had received the five talents went at once and traded with them, and he made five talents more. ^{17} So also he who had the two talents made two talents more. ^{18} But he who had received the one talent went and dug in the ground and hid his master's money." (Matt 25.14-17, 27-30 NKJV)

In this case, Jesus lauded the ones who invested, indicating that He approves of investment, particularly the right type of investment based upon Kingdom principles. On the other hand, He came down harshly on the one who did not invest. The non-investor did not lose anything; he simply did not do what God expected, which was to multiply whatever resources you have been given. Jesus said it is not good enough just to keep what you received; it must be invested in and bring a return. The story continues:

^{27} "Then you ought to have invested my money with the bankers, and at my coming, I should have received what was my own with interest. ^{28} So take the talent from him and give it to him who has the ten talents. ^{29} For to everyone who has will more be given, and he will have an abundance. But from the one who has not, even what he has will be taken away. ^{30} And cast the worthless servant into the outer darkness."

What you will notice about this story is that Jesus' focus was not on what amount was given for investment; His focus was

on what each did with their portfolio. God wants us all to be investors based on what He has given rather than the quantity of what we have been given. He clearly communicates that He expects everyone to invest as a principle. **Whatever God gives you, He expects you to produce a return. God is a God of increase; there is no reverse gear in the Kingdom, and the elevator in the Kingdom has no down button. We are programmed for increase.** It does not mean we will not have setbacks in life; it means that even when we have setbacks, we realize that our destiny is ahead, and we never settle for a setback. We always realize that the setback is an opportunity for a comeback because we do not belong in reverse. The Kingdom economy vehicle is an ATV (All-terrain vehicle). It can navigate hills and valleys, bad and good roads, but it keeps moving forward.

There are many types of investments available. A bank account and money in the bank is really not an investment in today's world. It is almost like the servant who did nothing with his money. The bank is like a black hole. Your money goes in, and it disappears into the abyss. The bank takes your money and invests it by giving loans and investing; they make a return on it but pay you little or no interest. In fact, banks often charge you for depositing the money that they use to make their money and give you no return at all. Find an investment that brings a return and increases your value.

We cannot go into detail on which investments are best, but each of us can do the research to determine which investment is best for us. Remember that the wealthiest people in the world are investors. This means we should familiarize ourselves with investment principles and opportunities and learn how to take advantage of opportunities. An investment can be something as simple as a child baking cookies and selling them to bring a financial return.

Some common investment types are:

MUTUAL FUNDS

INVESTMENT FUNDS

STOCKS AND BONDS

BUSINESS

ART

REAL ESTATE

KINGDOM (Invest in Missions, things that advance the Kingdom)

PENSIONS

IRA

401K

This list is by no means exhaustive, and I recommend that you do the research or speak with a financial advisor to determine what investment is best for you.

3. STEWARDSHIP

Dr. Myles Munroe made a statement that God does not bless you based on what you ask for; He blesses you based on how you managed the last blessing. God sometimes does not give you what you ask for; He gives you according to what you have shown you can successfully manage (parable of the talents). One of God's key metrics found throughout Jesus' discourse on Earth is faithfulness and stewardship. When the Bible says "well done, good and faithful servant," it is essentially saying well done to those who have been good stewards of what they have been given. The parable of the talents clearly demonstrates this. It does not matter what you have or how much you have. The question is, have you been a good steward of what you have? There are many people who are asking for more, but they have not been faithful over the little. Jesus made another statement in Luke 16:10-12:

10 "He who *is* faithful in *what is* least is faithful also in much; and he who is unjust in *what is* least is unjust also in much. **11** Therefore if you have not been faithful in the **unrighteous mammon,** who will commit to your trust the true *riches?* **12** And if you have not been faithful in what is another man's, who will give you what is your own?" (New King James Version) Faithfulness and stewardship are important to God.

Another statement that Jesus made is that whoever has, more will be given, and whoever does not have, even what he has, will be taken away. This statement sounds mean if you look at it from the surface, but Jesus was communicating a principle. Sometimes, the reason people have is because they know how to be good stewards, and so people seek out those who already have it because they have demonstrated they can manage what they have. The person who has had little and has squandered it, no one wants to give them anything because they know they will not be good stewards and will, in fact, waste the resources they have been given. Have you ever heard someone ask for a better house, but the house they are in, the windows are broken, the yard is unkept, and there is garbage piled up in the yard? Banks do not lend money to people who have not been good stewards of what they were entrusted previously. Credit scores track a person's steward-ship over their resources so that lenders can determine risk.

None of us will give to someone who has a track record of mis-managing their resources. If you think of it from a job perspec-tive, you do not get promoted for not showing up to work on time and not doing your job efficiently. You get more responsi-bilities when you have demonstrated that you can handle the first responsibilities you have been given. It is important that each of us maximize the resources and responsibilities we have in order to qualify for more. The bank gives you a bigger loan when they see that you have paid your last loan. The better you manage, the more you are rewarded; this is a principle.

I remember when my brother-in-law, who was a young Black man at the time, went to the bank to borrow money to finish his fledgling church. The project was very ambitious for a grow-ing congregation, but the bank was unwilling to lend them the money. After being rejected, instead of borrowing from the bank, they built out of pocket a great facility that consisted of a 1,000-seat sanctuary, an indoor gym, a bowling alley, and an indoor running track. The bank learned about what they had done and began pursuing them to borrow money. The same lender who would not entertain them is now begging them to borrow mon-ey. When they announced a new 5,000-seat facility, the bank came running and offered the most favorable terms.

One day, he and I were playing basketball, and we got a call that the bank wanted to meet with him. So he said we would leave and go to meet with the bankers. I asked him if we were going home to take a shower and change clothes before we went to the bank. He said, "No, we are going just as we are." He said,

"They would not pay attention to me when I showed up in a suit and tie, but now they will tolerate anything because they want our business." I sat in the banker's office laughing quietly as they went out of their way to offer us food and drinks. They acted polite despite the fact that we were sweaty and stinky. Even when people do not like you, they know the value of stewardship, and they probably said to themselves, if this man and his team could accomplish what they accomplished on their own, this is good ground for us to invest in. **Mark 4:25 NKJV: "For whoever has, to him more will be given; but whoever does not have, even what he has will be taken away from him."** What have you done with what you already have? If you want more, you should maximize what you have!

4. OWNERSHIP

One of the principles God emphasized to His people in the Book of Deuteronomy is the importance of ownership. He even made the statement, "You shall lend to other nations and will not borrow." You will be the lenders and not the borrowers. Ownership is a Kingdom principle. Consumers finance owners by continuing to consume and not own anything or very little. The Bible also tells us the borrower is essentially a slave to the lender. Rather than getting mad at lenders, why not become a lender? Instead of getting mad at business owners, why not become a business owner?

Ownership is power and leverage. Everyone seeks out owners. I saw an ad a few years back for a dinner with a presidential candidate in the United States. The ad was for a $ 250,000-a-plate dinner. I don't know about you, but I have been to many restaurants, and I have had expensive and exquisite meals, but I have never heard of a meal costing 250,000 dollars. Do you think they were selling a meal? No, these people were owners and lenders, and the politician was essentially selling influence because he knew the power of owners and ownership.

When you become an owner, your life changes. When you become an owner, there is a power shift and a paradigm shift. I recall that when I graduated from college and got married, I was working as a social worker, and my wife was pregnant and unemployed. When the deductions from my loans were completed every month, I only had $100 left. Being a young believer, I was bewildered and said to myself God must be punishing me. I wondered why I was in such a state when I was serving faithfully in my church and helping so many young people. I will never forget what happened one day when I was distressed about the situation. I came across a verse that stated that God will bless the works of your hands. I realized then that my hands were on the social work wheel, so I was getting a social work blessing. I decided then and there that I would change the situation and become an owner.

I sat down and started to think, and as I thought, I realized that every neighbor around me had a yard and their properties needed landscaping. I made a decision to sell my fairly new car and buy a truck and some lawn equipment. I employed a few young men from my youth ministry, and we formed Speedy Lawn Services. Needless to say, I was able to earn more than $100 at the end of the month. It was not easy; I would sometimes leave my social work job and go cut grass, rush home, take a shower, and then go back to work. This experience taught me the power of ownership. I went on to start a second business, which was a clothing company, then a third business, which was a computer company, and eventually a fourth business, which is a publishing company.

My businesses upgraded my income to the point where I was able to build my house, send my children to college with no loans, and give thousands to youth ministry projects because I was now an owner. I remember we would have youth conferences, and we would ask people for offerings, but we would not receive what we needed. I just wrote a check to make up the difference. The problem with most people is they never think of ownership in a world where getting a job and earning a salary is the default. Many young people, especially in minority and impoverished communities, are not exposed to ownership thinking and see very few models to pattern themselves after. This leads to a sense of fatalism where it appears that the only option is a job or some type of welfare.

Fortunately, I learned to think about ownership, so it was not difficult for me to transition. My father was a businessman, my uncles were businessmen, and many of my siblings were entrepreneurs, so it was not a stretch. After I wrote my first book and began to get royalties, I began to realize that the publishers were making most of the money, and I was getting 10%. If I began to publish my own materials, I could get a substantially higher percentage of the income, and this is what I did. After I began to publish my own books, others began to enquire how they could get their books published, and this is what caused One Rib Publications, my publishing company, to be born. Today, I have published over 1,000 books for authors in countries around the world, including Canada, Africa, Europe, the United States, and Europe, and I regularly receive royalties from my works.

To establish the Kingdom of God on Earth, we need more Kingdom people to be owners because owners are influencers. Influencers affect the behavior of society. If evil people are owners, then there will be more evil in the world. If good people are owners, then there will be more good people in the world. There is a principle in the Bible where God said to His people that they will lend and not borrow; they will be above and not beneath. The borrower is a slave to the lender, and we are not destined to be slaves. Owners are able to be benefactors; owners have tremendous power and influence for good. As Christians and citizens of the Kingdom of God, we are supposed to be owners and influencers. The mistake that many believers have made is to assume that there is something wrong with wealth and that we are supposed to be poor, suffering pilgrims while evil people prosper and dictate the terms of our lives. This is an absolute perversion of what God has said and implied in HIS WORD. Business is important to God, and it should be to us.

I believe strongly in promoting ownership and business. I created a conference for teenagers to teach them business rather than jobs. The conference is called iRise. At this conference, we will teach you how to start a business when you are a teenager. Every business is not a full-time business; there is something called a "side hustle" that you may do initially in your spare time to generate revenue. When it grows to the point that it contributes significantly to your financial upkeep, it can employ you. The book I wrote on this subject is "How to Start and Run a Business." It is a guide to the process of both starting and running a business. Prior to my employment in ministry, I ran a program for the government called the Small Business Center, where I advised clients on how to make business plans, budgets, cash flow projections, and loan proposals.

KEY KINGDOM ECONOMY PRINCIPLES

· When humans are not productive, they deteriorate physically, mentally, and spiritually.

· **Fruitful and multiplying also means engaging your God-given resources in a productive manner to fulfill His mandate.**

· The worst thing that can happen to a man (or woman) is to be idle.

· Productivity is essential to life in the Kingdom, which is why the Bible states that if a man does not work, he should not eat.

· **Whatever God gives you, He expects you to produce a return.**

· **God is a God of increase; there is no reverse gear in the Kingdom, and the elevator in the Kingdom has no down button. We are programmed for increase.**

· The Kingdom economy vehicle is an ATV (All-terrain vehicle); it can navigate hills and valleys, bad roads, and good ones, but it always keeps moving forward.

· **Investment is not about what you have; it is about what you do with what you have.**

NOTES

_____

_____

_____

_____

_____

_____

_____

_____

_____

_____

_____

_____

_____

_____

_____

CHAPTER 7:

MONEY MATTERS

So far, we have talked about a number of pertinent issues. In this chapter, we will delve into something that I call "Money Matters," pertinent issues relating to you and your money.

#1 MONEY AND MINISTRY – can't be separated. It takes money to do ministry, and anyone who says otherwise is either delusional or has never done ministry. **The lack of money is probably the greatest hindrance to effective ministry.** If the church operates in deficits or is poor, then its workers earn a low salary, and resources are lacking when it is time to help the poor. It is amazing that people will ask what the church is doing and, in the same breath, complain about the church receiving tithes and offerings.

Sometimes, attention is focused on a few mega-churches where pastors earn exorbitant sums, and this causes a distorted picture to form about the church and its role. The truth of the matter is that most pastors earn low salaries and have high demands, and most churches struggle to get by. The more money a church receives, the better it can assist members and the community. If they struggle to pay rent or mortgage, fewer resources are available to help those in need and provide essential services. The church is a helping institution, and the Kingdom of God is about helping. Jesus said, "If you have done it to the least of these, you have done it unto me" (Matt. 25.40). **Money and wealth on the Earth will either finance the truth or finance the lie.** The lies and evil programs are currently well outpacing the truth in the financing, meaning more people are being destroyed through drugs, pornography, suicide, and chaos. More money needs to be directed at solutions rather than the creation of problems.

#2 HONOR AND MONEY – In the Book of Proverbs, we are told to HONOR GOD with our wealth and the first fruits. Proverbs 3:9 k""Honor the Lord with your possessions, and with the first fruits of all your increase." (NKJV) This is not a suggestion; it is a statement about what is right and proper. Honor is about appreciation and gratitude. We are told to honor our parents. **What you do with your money is a sign of what you honor in your life.** Suppose you earn a salary or own a business. In that case, you can give ten percent into making your community better, feeding the poor, or ensuring that persons are inspired and motivated spiritually, or you can plunk it down in a strip club, throwing dollars in the air, and "make it rain" while a young stripper dances in front of you. If you do this, then your honor will be dedicated to mammon and perversion. I used to honor evil, but I have since changed allegiances and decided to honor God with my resources, knowing that it will help change lives. I give to the work of the Kingdom because I see lives changed and people rescued from crime, abuse, drug addiction, and destruction every day. I see dramatic improvements in the lives of the members of our church. Jesus said where your heart is, your treasure will follow. **It is not difficult to figure out what is important to you. Your money will speak.** If you love God and are dedicated to the Kingdom, you will honor God with whatever you earn or acquire. You cannot love God and His Kingdom and not give into the Kingdom; to not give and not give liberally is dishonoring God.

 # 3 MAKE SURE YOU HAVE A BUDGET – A budget is about stewardship. A budget helps you to manage your resources. A budget helps you to see a photograph of your financial status, whether you are spending more than you are earning or earning more than you are spending. A budget is essential for financial discipline. A budget also helps you to set financial priorities. For example, if you have a budget, you should deduct your fixed expenses before allocating money for non-essential purchases. You do not want to buy new clothes with the rent money or take your tithe money and go out for dinner or travel. Budgets help you maintain priorities. There are many budget tools out there that give sample budgets and templates that you can use. You can go online and select a budget tool to help you navigate the budget process.

 # 4 GENEROSITY – Generosity is a Kingdom characteristic. When you have the DNA of God, you are generous. You give without consternation. When you are driven by and influenced by Kingdom principles, you will give both cheerfully and abundantly. This is natural in the Kingdom. This scripture illuminates this important principle. **"The generous soul will be made rich, and he who waters will also be watered himself."**

Proverbs 11:25. God is a generous God, and He expects us to be generous. In my lifetime, my wife and I have given away four cars and donated thousands to various causes, especially youth work. We have paid for honeymoons for couples, trips, and hotels for others. We do it because this is the minimum that God expects, and as grateful people who are committed to Kingdom advancement, we know what the WORD says about the subject. I recall a recent experience my wife shared with me. She was at the gas station, and a lady pulled in and gave the gas attendant a one-dollar bill and some coins. She let him know that that was all she had. My wife saw what was happening and promptly reached into her wallet, paid for the gas, and gave the lady some cash to help her family. In the Kingdom, this is standard behavior.

 # 5 WEALTH GENERATORS – We have been given gifts and abilities that can generate wealth. These wealth generators are often hidden or undiscovered. Maybe you never realized that you could write a book or record music that could generate future wealth for you. Sometimes, we fail to develop hidden talents and bury or fail to recognize our wealth generators. That book that you did not write may have been a wealth generator. That idea that you dismissed may be a wealth generator. That talent that you failed to develop could have been a wealth generator.

#6 SOCIAL MEDIA AND MONEY – The world has changed, and one of the most impactful changes ever is the emergence of social media, not just as a tool of communication but as an income generator. There are so many options available, but it is undeniable how social media can impact your personal wealth. Let's just take a few examples:

YouTube – YouTube has leveled the playing field for unknown artists and individuals to have access to a global audience. One YouTube video can change your life forever from a financial perspective. Justin Beiber is a well-known example of someone who was unknown but came into immense wealth due to social media exposure. The wonderful thing about YouTube, Facebook, Instagram, and TikTok is that you can have a page or a channel at no cost. You then load content onto your page, and the content generates significant views for which you can get paid. Can you imagine you just create a clip on your phone, load it to YouTube, and that video goes viral, and you end up earning money for life? Facebook and the other available platforms have similar opportunities. Not everyone will be successful, but it certainly does not hurt to use a free resource that could possibly impact your financial future.

#7 MULTIPLE INCOME STREAMS – The days of giving your time and service to one company or entity are long gone. In a volatile world, diversification of income sources is essential for survival. A job is great, but there are so many ways to supplement your income that it would be foolish not to explore your options. I once had my job as my sole source of income until I realized that I did not have to be limited to my job, so I developed a part-time business, then I developed another part-time business, and then I wrote books that perpetually produced royalties, then I monetized my youtube channel. I now have multiple streams so that if one is down, the others can help pick up the slack. Of course, you must balance your work, business, and family. But if there is an opportunity, especially for passive income (income that pays you without you having to work directly), it is important to develop these opportunities. You never know which one will blow up, so it is better to have more seeds in the ground than less because something is bound to grow. The more seeds you have, the more growth opportunities you have.

My streams include:

Salary
Business Income
Royalties
Consulting Fees
Speaking Engagements
Social Media Income
Insurance Cash Values
Investments
Real Estate

8 CREDIT CARDS

Credit cards are a way of life in the times we live in. Everything revolves around credit cards. Whatever you want to do in life, a credit card is somehow involved. Credit cards can be good, bad, and ugly. **The key to credit cards is understanding the role of interest and staying on the right side of interest. The wrong side of interest is slavery; the right side of interest is benefits and returns.**

Credit cards are very convenient. If you need to book a hotel, purchase airline tickets, book a vacation, purchase something online, or rent a car, in most instances, a credit card is not an option; it is essential. The banks, credit card companies, and lending agencies make big money on credit cards, so they want you to get as many as possible and use them to the maximum level. A house loan or a car loan may fetch 4-10% interest, but a credit card can fetch up to 22% interest. If you borrow $20,000 for a car, the bank generates $1,000 to $2,000. If you have a credit card and you use $20,000, you could be paying $4,000 when you are on the wrong side of the interest equation. What is even worse is if you have a credit card with no benefits.

If you use credit cards, or should I say when you use credit cards, one of the keys is to limit interest exposure and maximize benefits. As a case in point, I have an American Airlines credit card that I use for business. If I purchase items using my credit cards and pay the card off within thirty days, I pay no interest, and I receive a return in terms of points that I can use for airline tickets, hotels, or products online. If I do not pay within 30 days, the interest kicks in. If you can help it, it is better to use your credit cards as a convenience rather than as a loan because the interest is high and becomes higher when penalties kick in. You could pay as much as 25% on some credit cards. One of the most important things you can do with excess cash is to pay down credit card debt to save on interest payments. On the other hand, when you have to use credit cards, use them in a way that allows you to accumulate benefits that you can redeem. I have traveled to many places, stayed in hotels, and achieved preferred status, including upgrades to first class, access to airline lounges and clubs, and exclusive benefits. Pay attention to benefits and interest rates whenever you are using credit cards. Always choose the cards with the best benefits and lowest interest rates.

One of the benefits that I now have is a lifetime platinum status on American Airlines after accumulating 2 million miles and points. This is a big deal. I never have to qualify again for platinum status. The higher your status is, the better your benefits will be. When you have status, you can pay for the same ticket as a non-status member or lower-level status member and receive a higher bonus. When I had gold status, each purchase and point achieved a 40-50% bonus. At my current status as Executive Platinum, I have achieved a 120% bonus. The higher you go, the more you are rewarded. As Jesus stated, "To him who has, more will be given." I also receive first-class upgrades up to 5 days ahead of travel, and when I show up on an upgrade list, I usually appear immediately at the top of the list. I have access to multiple airline clubs and lounges because of my American Airlines credit card or my American Express business platinum card. Make sure you use wisdom and do your research to gain maximum benefits.

#9 YOUR PERSONAL BRAND – Invest in yourself (increase your personal value) and build your brand. Think of yourself as a business or corporation. Every business has assets and liabilities; every business has a logo and a mission statement. Businesses invest in their brand to make it recognizable (Nike, Apple, Mercedes). Businesses and corporations seek to increase assets and reduce liabilities. Invest in yourself to increase your personal value; this may mean taking a course or doing research through Google or YouTube to learn something new. If you have one skill, this may mean adding a new skill. Learn how to market yourself effectively. Every business has a marketing budget. Learn how to present yourself to the world via social media or otherwise, which puts you in the best light and gives the public an insight into who you are and what you have to offer. Consider doing a video bio of yourself and an intro video. If you have services to offer, package them in a short clip so that persons who are interested can easily find out what you do. I once made a subtle change that increased my value significantly. I was a youth pastor for many years, and I found out that youth pastors were treated in an inferior way. I repackaged myself as a youth ministry specialist, which landed me consulting jobs for churches and denominations. The only thing that changed was my branding and presentation, which immediately increased my value.

KEY KINGDOM ECONOMY PRINCIPLES

- **MONEY AND MINISTRY** can't be separated. It takes money to do ministry, and anyone who says otherwise is either delusional or has never done ministry.

- **The lack of money is probably the greatest hindrance to effective ministry.**

- **Money and wealth on the Earth will either finance the truth or finance the lie.**

- **What you do with your money is a sign of what you honor in your life.**

- **It is not difficult to figure out what is important to you. Your money will speak.**

- Generosity is a Kingdom characteristic.

- Every one of us has been given gifts and abilities that can generate wealth.

- Social media can impact (generate) your personal wealth.

NOTES

CHAPTER 8:

WHAT MONEY CANNOT ANSWER

One of the greatest mistakes the world and the church have made is to have faith in money. We often make this statement that "Money answers all things." Does money really answer all things? There is a passage in the Bible that says money answers all things, but common sense should tell us there is a context for those words because there are some things in life for which money offers no answer.

The truth is money answers some questions but is powerless in other cases. If you have an electric bill, a car loan, or a mortgage, money can answer those questions fairly easily. The problem begins when we start looking at intangible items. Money is great for goods and services, but issues of the soul and even the body have little respect for money.

If you are sick, money can buy you healthcare, but it cannot buy you health. You can have the best doctors in the world, but there are healing mechanisms built into your body that only God can activate. If those healing properties are not activated, you can spend your life savings, but there is still no answer. I recall several years ago, the founder of Apple Computers, Steve Jobs, was ill with cancer. If anyone could buy health, it would have been him. Although he had billions of dollars at his disposal and the best that medicine could offer, his money was not good enough, and he died because money could not answer health. Money can buy medicine but not health. Health comes from God.

Money can't buy you peace of mind. Money can buy you a comfortable space but not a comfortable mind. Money can buy you a vacation, but it cannot ease your depression. Ever wonder why rich people commit suicide just like the poor? It is because neither the wealth of the rich nor the poverty of the poor can buy peace of mind. Money can buy you a piece of property or pieces of property, but it cannot buy you peace of mind or sanity. Money cannot even buy sleep. The very famous singer that we referred to as the "King of Pop," Michael Jackson, made millions of dollars and had the best doctors in the world but still could not sleep. He died trying to find sleep. He paid a doctor to give him drugs normally reserved for anaesthetic patients, and yet, with all of that, he never got the sleep he so desperately wanted. It caused me to realize the value of a good night's sleep. I thank God I have never had a problem sleeping.

Money can buy happiness, but it cannot buy joy. Money can buy you things that will give you temporary pleasure but not joy that lasts a lifetime. There was a billionaire who lived decades ago, and in spite of all his money, he could not buy happiness or sanity. Eventually, he would not shave, brush his teeth, or allow people in his presence. He died as a very wealthy, insane person. Money can buy you a house, but it cannot buy you a home. Some people have a twenty-two-bedroom house with a full-time butler, but they do not sleep in the same room with their wives, and their children hate them. Money can buy you children, but it cannot buy you a family. You can literally buy children today, but you cannot buy a family.

God's economy and commonwealth go far beyond money. We know that God is King of Kings, Lord of Lords, Omniscient, and Omnipresent. He is the great one that sustains us all. He sets up systems and tears them down. He issues laws and decrees, and they are established forever. It would be good and important to know if there was a system He set up for our benefit. Let us take a look at His economic plan.

His economy (system) is different from world economies. He lets us know that His system is different and advises us not to conform to the "world's" system. Romans 12: "I beseech you therefore, brethren, by the mercies of God, that you present your bodies a living sacrifice, holy, acceptable to God, which is your reasonable service. 2 And do not be conformed to this world, but be transformed by the renewing of your mind, that you may prove what is that good and acceptable and perfect will of God..."

World economies are failing today because they are primarily built around the acquisition and storage of money. Money is important, but wealth is more important than money. Wealth does not have to mean money; it can mean access to things people usually pay for. You can be wealthy in houses and land without ever having money. One dictionary definition of wealth states, "marked by abundance." This is the type of terminology that Jesus used. Instead of telling us we would have a rich life and many things, Jesus said we would have an "Abundant Life."

Sometimes, we make the mistake of believing that rich people are the money offenders. The reality is that poor people and rich people offend to the same extent. The poor man complains about the rich man but sells his child to get money. Think about what happens when you give a poor man money. Do they treat money differently than the rich? Do they take their money and help their friends who are down and out? In most cases, they do the same thing that rich people do; they spend it on themselves, or they hoard it and become obsessed with getting more. Many poor people quickly go broke when they acquire money because they never understood the value of it and end up consuming it all rather than investing it.

The world that we will live in is obsessed with obtaining money, spending money, and, many times worshiping money. I heard a statement once made by Dr. Myles Munroe and others. It stated, "Poor people spend money, rich people hoard money, wealthy people invest money." You can tell the category a person is in by how they approach money. Jesus spoke quite a bit about money, but His conversations and teachings about money often introduced concepts that went against what people considered the norm. God emphasizes the proper role of money throughout the Bible.

What may seem like it does not make sense in the parable of the talents is that Jesus says to him, "He who has, more will be given." The point He was actually making is that God is a God of wealth, and He encourages productivity and investment. If you are unproductive, He indicates that you are punished, and if you are productive, you are given more to continue to reproduce. I learnt a lesson about this principle as I began to increase in business. When you get to a higher level, you are given more than you were given at a lower level. I am currently an executive platinum member of the American Airlines rewards program. When you are gold, you get a 50% bonus, but when you reach platinum status, it jumps to 80%. When you get to executive platinum status, it jumps all the way to 120%. The higher I go, the more benefits I get. This is a principle of life: when you have, you receive more because the owners or resources trust people who have proven to be good stewards.

The problem with many poor people is not money; it is mentality. Many people do not grow up with an attitude of ownership. They grow up with a consumer mentality, so whatever they have is quickly consumed, and they are in search of more to consume. This was one of the points vividly explained in a book titled, "Rich Dad, Poor Dad." Jesus wants us to think differently than we are accustomed to. He says to be faithful and invest the little you have the same way the wealthy invest their wealth.

Your faith should never follow your money; your money should follow your faith (treasure). Money is supposed to be a servant, not a master. Money is there to meet needs and to answer the questions it can answer. Money was meant to be distributed and circulated rather than hoarded. What good is it if you have money that sits in a vault while there are people with great needs that you can help? Proverbs 10:22 states, "The blessing of the Lord makes one rich, and He adds no sorrow with it."

Wealth is not supposed to bring sorrow, regret, or stress. The greatest problem with money in the world is misunderstanding the purpose of money. Jesus said, "Give, and it shall be given back to you." This does not make sense to the average person, but it is a part of God's system. Seedtime and harvest and replenish are eternal principles. If you give, it will be returned to you. **It** is important never to confuse wealth with excess. Wealth is fine, but excess can be harmful. The dictionary indicates that excess is "Exceeding a normal, usual, reasonable, or proper limit. ex•ces sive•ly adv. ex•ces sive•ness n. Synonyms: excessive, exorbitant, extravagant, immoderate, the state of exceeding what is normal or sufficient: rains that filled the reservoirs to excess. 2. An amount or quantity beyond what is normal or sufficient."

If you have 21 cars but no one drives them, or if you have 18 houses and no one lives in them, this is excess. Money is meant to circulate and to serve us and not for us to serve it. When money stops circulating, it causes financial constipation and mental illness. Constipation can be a painful and unproductive condition. It stops the proper flow and causes a backup that produces disease and discomfort. Financial constipation causes the same strains and pains as physical constipation.

The Book of Acts shows how money and wealth and God's economy should work. "Now the multitude of those who believed were of one heart and one soul; neither did anyone say that any of the things he possessed was his own, but they had all things in common. 33 And with great power, the apostles gave witness to the resurrection of the Lord Jesus. And great grace was upon them all. 34 Nor was there anyone among them who lacked; for all who were possessors of lands or houses sold them, and brought the proceeds of the things that were sold, 35 and laid them at the apostles' feet; and they distributed to each as anyone had need."

The greatest money problem is when the wrong people possess it. The problem with money is when it becomes a treasure. Treasure is not supposed to be accumulated or stored as wealth in the form of money, jewels, or other valuables. Treasure is supposed to be valuable or precious possessions that accomplish God's purpose in your life. Do not seek money; seek treasure. Do not seek to be rich; seek to be wealthy. Learn to prioritize your pursuits: "Seek first the Kingdom."

Be careful about what you possess and what possesses you (check yourself). Remember the example of the Apostle Paul and understand the value of contentment in all situations: Philippians 4: 11 "Not that I speak in regard to need, for I have learned in whatever state I am, to be content: 12 I know how to be abased, and I know how to abound. Everywhere and in all things, I have learned both to be full and to be hungry, both to abound and to suffer need. 13 I can do all things through Christ who strengthens me…19 And my God shall supply all your need according to His riches in glory by Christ Jesus."

KEY KINGDOM ECONOMY PRINCIPLES

· There is a passage in the Bible that says money answers all things, but common sense should tell us there is a context for those words because there are some things in life for which money offers no answer.

· **Your faith should never follow your money; your money should follow your faith (treasure).**

· Money can buy you a comfortable space but not a comfortable mind.

· It is important never to confuse wealth with excess. Wealth is fine, but excess can be harmful.

- The problem with many poor people is not money; it is mentality.

- Money is supposed to be a servant, not a master.

- **It is important never to confuse wealth with excess. Wealth is fine, but excess can be harmful.**

NOTES

CHAPTER 9:

MONEY, WEALTH, KNOWLEDGE AND WISDOM

The Bible tells us that people perish without knowledge and wisdom. It is vital that we study the world's economic system and acquire knowledge that will increase our value. The more you know, the more you will get paid. Knowledge is power. Today, "digital" opportunities are growing. Knowledge about AI (artificial intelligence) is changing the game. Get knowledge about current trends and opportunities. Do not be on the wrong side of the future. Pursue knowledge, whether formal or informal.

Wisdom is also power because wisdom is known as the principal need of man. **Knowledge can be acquired from study and books, but God gives wisdom to those who ask.** God does not give away money. He gives us ideas, inventions, and strategies to cause wealth that already exists to manifest. He rewards both faithfulness and fruitfulness. **If you want a reward from God, become faithful and fruitful.** He gives us the power to get wealth rather than granting us wealth. We use His wisdom and the power that He gave us to accomplish exploits that benefit the world through the Kingdom economy. **Do not tell God what to do or how to do it; make your request and watch Him work.**

He promised to make us plentiful in goods and indicated that He wanted us to have an abundant life. The idea that He would want others to benefit from what He created and His own citizens and children to be deprived is lacking in insight and awareness and anchored in ignorance of His own pronouncements. When speaking to the children of Israel, He said He would lead them from bondage into a land flowing with milk and honey. Milk and honey are reflective of abundance and satisfaction, not deprivation or meager existence. Not only that, but He also indicated in the Book of Deuteronomy that we would be the head and not the tail, above and not beneath, and we would be blessed going out and coming in.

To do well and have wealth is not anti-Kingdom. It only becomes anti-Kingdom if our wealth is used for carnal consumption. Never for one second or milliliter of a second do I ever consider anything other than God wants me to prosper. I realize that we have an adversary, as Jesus clearly stated, who does not want us to succeed, but God wants us to succeed. Life often goes in the seasons, and conditions in the world ebb and flow. The Apostle Paul spoke of times when he was abounding and other times when he was abasing (suffering lack). Never stop sowing seed even when you are not seeing immediate results because it is a principle. I went through periods of great business profits, but I also encountered seasons of loss. Through every phase, I stuck with the principles rather than changing based on the current environment or season.

It is true that the Disciples sacrificed to follow Jesus and may not have been wealthy, but neither were they poor or destitute. We must remember that Jesus had a treasurer in Judas who was stealing from the treasury, and it went unnoticed, so there must have been substantial money in the treasury. Jesus and His team traveled extensively and were provided for. We must remember that the scripture says that He became poor so that we could be rich. We live in the world, not outside of it. Conditions in the world, the environment, and our local and global economy affect our status, but we are not limited only to our environment. God has promised to bless us in spite of external circumstances and economies.

Wealth is not just having money and possessing lands. Wealth is also access. If you do not own a car but have access to one, the access puts you in a position of wealth. If you don't own a house but are living in a house without paying for it because you were given access, you are still wealthy. Persons who complain or have the opinion that Kingdom citizens should not be wealthy are saying the devil and those evil persons under his influence should have it instead. I heard a conversation the other day where a young man was complaining that a pastor was driving a 5-year-old BMW and did not have a problem with a Basketball player having five Rolls Royce and earning 50 million dollars a year.

The Bible actually indicates that it is important for believers to participate in "giving and receiving" with their pastors. The scripture also indicates that a workman is worthy of his hire, meaning a pastor or leader should be paid adequately for the service they provide. To consider otherwise would be an incredible abuse and insult to God's servants and shepherds. They should not do the opposite and accumulate excessive wealth using resources that are designed to help their congregation. We must remember that God said it is your father's good pleasure to give you the Kingdom. The Bible also tells us that the wealth of the wicked is laid up for the just. This means that the wicked who use wealth wrongly will end up with their wealth being redirected to those who will do good with it. This is the way the Kingdom economy works; you are rewarded for doing good with your wealth. The job of the devil is to keep wealth away from those who would do good with it, and our job is to obey Kingdom principles and not consume it on lust.

There is not one scripture in the Bible where God promised poverty. Poverty is against His nature. He stated in Jeremiah, "I know the plans I have for you, plans for you to prosper and see a good end." **It is a reasonable expectation of the righteous to be blessed so that they can advance the Kingdom and establish the covenant.** God makes a way when the devil tries to deprive us. One interesting scenario is that while Paul was under house arrest, he was allowed visitors and lived much better than other prisoners. It is indicated that he may have even had servants while in prison. No matter the condition or the situation, we deserve the best in favor and preferential treatment.

One of the keys to wealth is learning to serve your gift for free before seeking remuneration. This is a seed into the future that you want. There were many times I offered my services to local schools, various communities, or church groups with no immediate return, but the return came from my gift being exposed. The free opportunities also resulted in book sales and exposure to my other products and materials. **Do not just sit and wait for money; make Kingdom money moves.**

It would be wisdom for us all to consider the following action steps:

1. COMMIT TO SEEKING AND PRIORITIZING THE KINGDOM FIRST (as Jesus commanded)

2. COMMIT TO THE KINGDOM ECONOMIC MODEL (and not be snared by the world's system)

3. COMMIT TO ADVANCING THE KINGDOM

4. COMMIT TO GIVING AND RECEIVING AS A WAY OF LIFE

Remember that everything for Earth is on Earth already. The only things that need to happen and that need to be met are movements and shifts. Whether we achieve our wealth and money goals or not, our trust should remain in God and not mammon. No matter what happens, trust God and His word regardless of what you see.

Do not sacrifice your children or family in the pursuit of wealth. Your children, spouse, and family are much more valuable than any resources you accumulate. It is sometimes better to take less so that you can have more time with your family. My wife gave up a high-paying executive position as an insurance company Vice President to manage our family business for a fifty percent lower salary. Initially, it was difficult, but it turned out to be one of our best decisions. Both our family and our business prospered because of putting God and family first.

Remember to duplicate principles and not experiences. Some times, we hear a great testimony about someone else's journey and try to duplicate that person's experience. We should learn principles that we can incorporate into our experience rather than attempting to incorporate other people's experiences into our experience.

KEY KINGDOM ECONOMY PRINCIPLES

- Knowledge can be acquired from study and books, but God gives wisdom to those who ask.

- If you want a reward from God, become faithful and fruitful.

- Do not tell God what to do or how to do it; make your request and watch Him work.

- To do well and have wealth is not anti-Kingdom.

- There is not one scripture in the Bible where God promised poverty.

- It is a reasonable expectation of the righteous to be blessed so that they can advance the Kingdom and establish the covenant.

- Do not just sit and wait for money; make Kingdom money moves.

NOTES

CHAPTER 10:

KINGDOM ECONOMY SCRIPTURES

2 Cor 8:9

"For you know the grace of our Lord Jesus Christ, that though He was rich, yet for your sake, He became poor so that you through **His poverty** might become rich."

Proverbs 19:1

"Better is a poor man who walks in his integrity than a rich man who is crooked in his ways."

1 Samuel 2:8

"He raises up the poor from the dust; he lifts the needy from the ash heap to make them sit with princes and inherit a seat of honor. For the pillars of the earth are the Lord's, and on them he has set the world."

Proverbs 11:25

"The generous soul will be made rich, And he who waters will also be watered himself."

Leviticus 19:34

"The foreigner residing among you must be treated as your native-born. Love them as yourself, for you were foreigners in Egypt. I am the Lord your God."

Isiah 63.13

"Therefore thus says the Lord GOD: "Behold, My servants shall eat, But you shall be hungry; Behold, My servants shall drink, But you shall be thirsty; Behold, My servants shall rejoice, But you shall be ashamed;"

Proverbs 11:24 (NKJV)

"There is one who scatters, yet increases more; And there is one who withholds more than is right, But it leads to poverty."

2 Corinthians 9:7

"So let each one give as he purposes in his heart, not grudgingly or of necessity; for God loves a cheerful giver."

Deuteronomy 15:1-5

"At the end of every seven years, you must cancel debts. This is how it is to be done: Every creditor shall cancel any loan they have made to a fellow Israelite. They shall not require payment from anyone among their own people because the Lord's time for canceling debts has been proclaimed…there need be no poor people among you, for in the land the Lord your God is giving you to possess as your inheritance, he will richly bless you if only you fully obey the Lord your God and are careful to follow all these commands I am giving you today."

Leviticus 25:35

"If your brother becomes poor and cannot maintain himself with you, you shall support him as though he were a stranger and a sojourner, and he shall live with you."

Proverbs 31:8-9

"Speak up for those who cannot speak for themselves, for the rights of all who are destitute. Speak up and judge fairly; defend the rights of the poor and needy."

Proverbs 22:22-23

"Do not rob the poor, because he is poor, or crush the afflicted at the gate, for the Lord will plead their cause and rob of life those who rob them."

Proverbs 21:13

"Those who shut their ears to the cries of the poor will be ignored in their own time of need."

2 Corinthians 8:12

"For if there is first a willing mind, it is accepted according to what one has, and not according to what he does not have."

Luke 12:32-34

"Fear not, little flock, for it is your Father's good pleasure to give you the kingdom. Sell your possessions, and give to the needy. Provide yourselves with moneybags that do not grow old, with a treasure in the heavens that does not fail, where no thief approaches and no moth destroys. For where your treasure is, there will your heart be also."

1 John 3:17

"But if anyone has the world's goods and sees his brother in need, yet closes his heart against him, how does God's love abide in him?"

Proverbs 19:1

"Better is a poor man who walks in his integrity than a rich man who is crooked in his ways."

1 Samuel 2:8

"He raises up the poor from the dust; he lifts the needy from the ash heap to make them sit with princes and inherit a seat of honor. For the pillars of the earth are the Lord's, and on them he has set the world."

Leviticus 19:34

"The foreigner residing among you must be treated as your native-born. Love them as yourself, for you were foreigners in Egypt. I am the Lord your God."

Deuteronomy 15:1-5

"At the end of every seven years, you must cancel debts. This is how it is to be done: Every creditor shall cancel any loan they have made to a fellow Israelite. They shall not require payment from anyone among their own people, because the Lord's time for canceling debts has been proclaimed…there need be no poor people among you, for in the land the Lord your God is giving you to possess as your inheritance, he will richly bless you, if only you fully obey the Lord your God and are careful to follow all these commands I am giving you today."

Proverbs 21:13

"Those who shut their ears to the cries of the poor will be ignored in their own time of need."

Luke 12:32-34

"Fear not, little flock, for it is your Father's good pleasure to give you the kingdom. Sell your possessions, and give to the needy. Provide yourselves with moneybags that do not grow old, with a treasure in the heavens that does not fail, where no thief approaches and no moth destroys. For where your treasure is, there will your heart be also."

1 John 3:17

"But if anyone has the world's goods and sees his brother in need, yet closes his heart against him, how does God's love abide in him?"

2 Corinthians 9:11

"While you are enriched in everything for all liberality, which causes thanksgiving through us to God."

Luke 6:38

"Give, and it will be given to you: good measure, pressed down, shaken together, and running over will be put into your bosom.

For with the same measure that you use, it will be measured back to you."

2 Corinthians 8:12

"For if there is first a willing mind, it is accepted according to what one has, and not according to what he does not have."

Psalm 112:5

"A good man deals graciously and lends; He will guide his affairs with discretion."

2 Corinthians 9:10

"Now may He who supplies seed to the sower, and bread for food, supply and multiply the seed you have sown and increase the fruits of your righteousness."

Luke 6:30

"Give to everyone who asks of you. And from him who takes away your goods do not ask them back."

Isaiah 40:29

"He gives power to the weak, and to those who have no might He increases strength."

James 1:5

"If any of you lacks wisdom, let him ask of God, who gives to all liberally and without reproach, and it will be given to him."

2 Corinthians 9:6

"But this I say: He who sows sparingly will also reap sparingly, and he who sows bountifully will also reap bountifully."

Luke 11:13

"If you then, being evil, know how to give good gifts to your children, how much more will your heavenly Father give the Holy Spirit to those who ask Him!"

Matt. 17:27

"Nevertheless, lest we offend them, go to the sea, cast in a hook, and take the fish that comes up first. And when you have opened its mouth, you will find a piece of money; take that and give it to them for Me and you."

Matt 25.14-18, 27-30

"For it will be like a man going on a journey, who called his servants[a] and entrusted to them his property. 15 To one he gave five talents,[b] to another two, to another one, to each according to his ability. Then he went away. 16 He who had received the five talents went at once and traded with them, and he made five talents more. 17 So also he who had the two talents made two talents more. 18 But he who had received the one talent went and dug in the ground and hid his master's money."

27 Then you ought to have invested my money with the bankers, and at my coming I should have received what was my own with interest. 28 So take the talent from him and give it to him who has the ten talents. 29 For to everyone who has will more be given, and he will have an abundance. But from the one who has not,

even what he has will be taken away. ³⁰ And cast <u>the worthless servant</u> into the outer darkness.

Matt 6:19-24

¹⁹ "Do not lay up for yourselves treasures on earth, where moth and rust destroy and where thieves break in and steal; ²⁰ but lay up for yourselves treasures in heaven, where neither moth nor rust destroys and where thieves do not break in and steal. ²¹ For where your treasure is, there your heart will be also. "No one can serve two masters; for either he will hate the one and love the other, or else he will be loyal to the one and despise the other. You cannot serve God and mammon. ²² "The lamp of the body is the eye. If therefore your eye is good, your whole body will be full of light. ²³ But if your eye is bad, your whole body will be full of darkness. If therefore the light that is in you is darkness, how great *is* that darkness! ²⁴ "No one can serve two masters; for either he will hate the one and love the other, or else he will be loyal to the one and despise the other. You cannot serve God and mammon.

Proverbs 6:9 - 11

"How long will you sleep, O sluggard? When will you arise out of your sleep? Yet, a little sleep, a little slumber, a little folding of the hands to rest; So shall your poverty come as one who travels, and your want like an armed man."

Proverbs 14:23

"All hard work brings a profit, but mere talk leads only to poverty."

Proverbs 10:15

"The rich man's wealth is his fortress, the ruin of the poor is their poverty."

Proverbs 11:24

"One man gives freely, yet gains even more; another withholds unduly, but comes to poverty."

Deuteronomy 28:12 (New King James Version)

"The Lord will open to you His good treasure, the heavens, to give the rain to your land in its season, and to bless all the work of your hand. You shall lend to many nations, but you shall not borrow."

NOTES